THIS LAND CALLED AMERICA: **DELAWARE**

CREATIVE EDUCATION

Published by Creative Education

P.O. Box 227, Mankato, Minnesota 56002

Creative Education is an imprint of The Creative Company

www.thecreativecompany.us

Book and cover design by Blue Design (www.bluedes.com)

Art direction by Rita Marshall

Printed in the United States of America

Photographs by Alamy (PHOTOTAKE Inc., Stock Connection Distribu-
tion, Maximilian Weinzierl), Corbis (Bill Barksdale, Kevin Fleming, Philip
Scalia), Getty Images (Cornell Capa//Time Life Pictures, Jeff Foott,
Allan Grant//TimeLife Pictures, C. E. Lewis/U.S. Air Force, MPI, David
Muench, Jake Rajs, Stock Montage, Time Life Pictures/Mansell/Time
Life Pictures, Vintage Images, Scott Warren/Aurora)

Library of Congress Cataloging-in-Publication Data

Wimmer, Teresa.

Delaware / by Teresa Wimmer.

p. cm. — (This land called America)

Includes bibliographical references and index.

ISBN 978-1-58341-633-4

1. Delaware—Juvenile literature. I. Title. II. Series.

F164.3.W55 2008

975.1—dc22   2007015003

First Edition

9 8 7 6 5 4 3 2 1

This Land Called America

DELAWARE

Teresa Wimmer

Show

Delaware

TERESA WIMMER

EACH SUMMER, AS THE WEATHER TURNS HOT AND MUGGY, PEOPLE FROM ALL OVER AMERICA FLOCK TO DELAWARE'S BEACHES TO COOL OFF. THEY WALK ALONG THE BOARDWALK EATING COTTON CANDY, TAKE A DIP IN THE ATLANTIC OCEAN, OR BUILD SAND CASTLES. THEY CAN FEEL THE SALTY WATER RUSH BETWEEN THEIR TOES IF THEY GET CLOSE ENOUGH TO THE OCEAN. ON THE BEACHES WHERE TOURISTS DON'T GO, DELAWAREANS WALK IN THE WIND ALONG THE SAND DUNES OR FISH IN THE OCEAN. SANDPIPERS AND OTHER SHOREBIRDS PROBE THE SAND FOR CRAB EGGS TO EAT. IN THE SMALL STATE OF DELAWARE, A DAY AT THE BEACH IS NEVER FAR AWAY.

YEAR
1610 British captain Samuel Argall names Delaware's bay, first discovered by Henry Hudson, De La Warr Bay.
EVENT

Battle for the Bay

In 1609, a Dutch explorer named Henry Hudson sailed into Delaware Bay. He did not stay, but he told people back home in the Netherlands about the many different animals and lush green lands that he saw there. More Dutch people sailed to Delaware in 1631. They founded a settlement and named it Zwaanendael, which means "Valley of the Swans."

Henry Hudson

When the Dutch landed, they encountered the Lenape, Susquehannock, and Nanticoke American Indian tribes. For thousands of years, the men had hunted animals such as foxes, beavers, and raccoons, and the women had grown crops such as corn, beans, and squash. The natives taught the Dutch how to grow these crops, and the Dutch traded furs with the Indians.

In 1638, Swedish people landed in Delaware and built a settlement. They named it Fort Christina, after their queen back home. They planted tobacco and traded for furs with the Indians. They built the first log cabins in the United States.

Dutch explorer Henry Hudson (above) received a warm welcome from the American Indians he encountered in Delaware (opposite).

The Dutch and Swedes fought constantly over who would control the Delaware River and Delaware Bay. The Dutch took Delaware from the Swedes in 1655. Later, the British took the land from the Dutch.

Before he could take over Pennsylvania, Penn had to make an agreement with the natives.

In 1681, an Englishman named William Penn was given a piece of land by England's King Charles II that he named Pennsylvania. But he wanted access to the Atlantic Ocean, too, so the Dutch gave him Delaware as well. Penn belonged to a religious group called the Quakers. He wanted his new land to be a peaceful and friendly place. He divided Delaware into three counties and kept them under his control.

The people in the three Delaware counties made a good living. They grew wheat, rye, and corn. Some raised cattle, and some even owned slaves from Africa. In the northern county, named New Castle, mills sprang

Quakers such as William Penn have always believed in dressing in plain, simple clothes.

up along the rivers. The mills turned lumber into paper and wheat into flour. The people of Delaware prospered so much that they wanted to separate from Pennsylvania. They wanted to have their own government and laws.

YEAR

1704   Delaware's legislature meets independently for the first time.

EVENT

- *9* -

In 1776, the 13 American colonies declared their independence from England. They fought the Revolutionary War and gained the right to govern themselves. The people in Delaware took the opportunity to also declare their independence from Pennsylvania. In 1787, the U.S. Constitution was drawn up, but it had to be accepted by all of the states. On December 7, 1787, Delaware became the first state to ratify, or accept, the Constitution. Delaware was nicknamed "The First State."

After achieving statehood, Delaware attracted many people from countries such as Germany, Ireland, Poland, and Italy. They farmed the rich soil and started many companies and industries. They pushed the American Indians farther west, until only a few remained in southern Delaware. Early settlements grew into such cities as Wilmington and Newark.

In the mid-1900s, many people and businesses moved to Wilmington's suburbs. The downtown area became neglected. To bring people back, Wilmington's leaders began a program that sold older downtown homes cheaply to anyone who would refurbish and live in them. They also made it inexpensive for new businesses to come to Delaware.

People have canoed the Delaware River for pleasure since the 19th century (opposite), sometimes spotting beavers (above) along the way.

YEAR

1769   Newark Academy, which is later renamed the University of Delaware, is founded.

EVENT

- 10 -

Water, Marshes, and Chickens

DELAWARE IS A THIN STRIP OF LAND WHOSE EASTERN
BORDER IS DELAWARE BAY. MARYLAND IS ITS NEIGHBOR
TO THE SOUTH AND WEST. THE NORTHERN BORDER OF
DELAWARE, IN THE SHAPE OF A SEMICIRCLE, COMES
INTO CONTACT WITH THE SOUTHEASTERN CORNER OF
PENNSYLVANIA. AT ITS BROADEST POINT, DELAWARE IS

State bird: blue hen chicken

only 39 miles (63 km) wide. That is smaller than many counties in other U.S. states.

Most of Delaware lies in the low, flat lands of the Atlantic Coastal Plain. Delaware is closer to sea level than any state except Florida. During the summer, Rehoboth Beach calls to many people all along the Atlantic Coast. Rehoboth means "open spaces," but there are not many open spaces in the summer. The town's population swells from 1,500 to 50,000 due to summer vacationers.

In the southern part of the state, the Delaware River carries lots of sand through Delaware Bay. The sand gets blown into hill-like dunes along the beaches. A good place to see the dunes is Cape Henlopen State Park. It features the Great Dune, which is 80 feet (24 m) tall. During World War II, military bunkers were built in the dunes because the dunes were such good hiding places.

The shores along Delaware Bay are muddy, flat, and covered by grassy saltwater marshes.

Soggy marshes and wetlands cover much of the southern part of the state. The biggest marshy area is called Great Cypress Swamp. Skinny cypress trees grow there. The Patriarch Tree is in the Great Cypress Swamp. It is more than 600 years old and is believed to be the oldest tree in the state.

YEAR
1802   E. I. du Pont builds a gunpowder mill along Brandywine Creek, beginning the DuPont empire.
EVENT

Delaware's coastline and waterways provide many spots for birds to stop during their travels. Bombay Hook National Wildlife Refuge is a wetland area that is home to many birds, such as bald eagles and egrets. Turtles and frogs also live there. Each winter, more than 100,000 snow geese migrate to the refuge to live. More snow geese live around Bombay Hook than anywhere else in North America.

Egrets, herons, and other shorebirds enjoy feasting on the many fish in Delaware Bay. People love the delicious fish, too. Fishermen harvest seafood from Delaware Bay and ship it to stores and restaurants all over the world.

Delaware's 15,978-acre (6,466 ha) Bombay Hook National Wildlife Refuge, established in 1937, protects snow geese (opposite) as well as frogs (above).

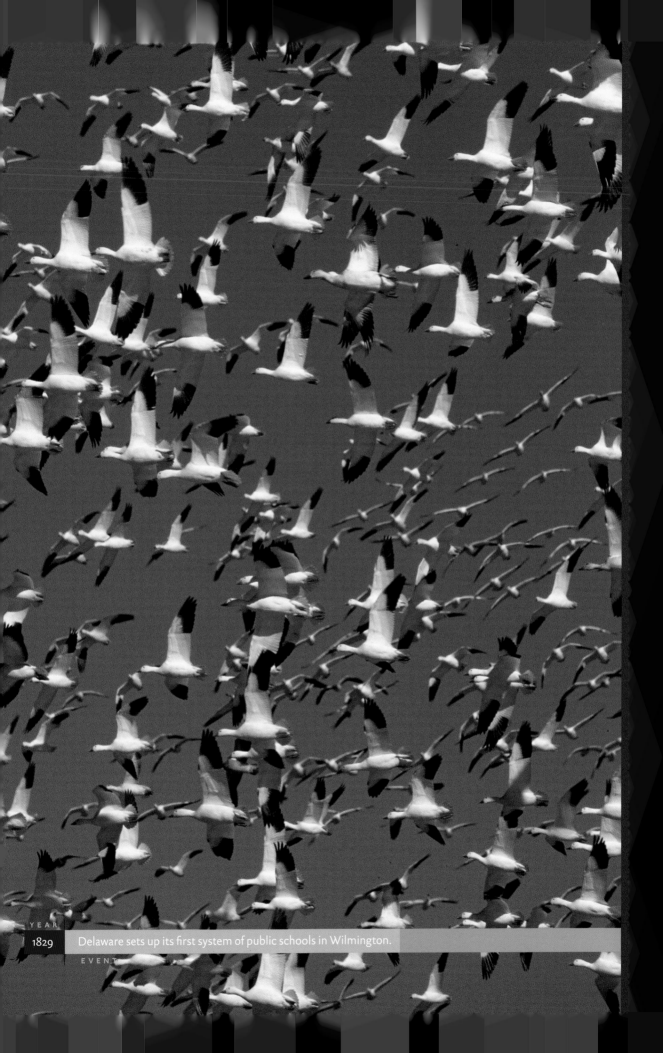

1829 Delaware sets up its first system of public schools in Wilmington.

Bald cypress swamps
are common in the
southeastern U.S., but
they can be found as far
north as Delaware.

The southern half of Delaware is covered with woodlands and farms. People here grow soybeans and corn and raise dairy cattle. Another important product of this region is the broiler chicken. The first broiler chickens were raised in Delaware in the early 1920s by accident. Today, broiler chickens account for half of the state's agricultural income.

In the northern part of the state, the Brandywine Creek winds through valleys and hills dotted with trees. Each fall, the green trees turn into vibrant shades of red, orange, and yellow. Delaware's largest city, Wilmington, lies along Brandywine Creek. The area is home to most of Delaware's industrial and manufacturing companies. The factories produce such items as chemicals, processed foods, paper products, and transportation equipment.

Throughout most of Delaware, the weather is moderate. The ocean breezes keep the air pleasantly cool in summer, with an average temperature of 75 °F (24 °C), and mildly warm in winter. Farther inland, summers can be hot and humid and winters colder with snow and sleet. But for the most part, the people of Delaware enjoy good weather.

YEAR

1861–1865   Delaware soldiers fight mainly on the Union side during the Civil War.

EVENT

When Europeans came
to Delaware, they built
more permanent houses
(opposite) than natives
such as the Nanticoke
(pictured) had.

Home to a Few

Many different Indian tribes once lived in Delaware. The Nanticoke and Susquehannock hunted Delaware's woods and fished its rivers. The Lenape lived there, too. The Nanticoke and Lenape were peaceful. The Susquehannock constantly tried to take land away from them.

Annie Jump Cannon
(opposite) also received
a master's degree in
science from Oxford
University.

Lenape chief Tishcohan's
treaty with William Penn
enabled more settlers to
stay in Delaware.

Soon, settlers from Germany, Ireland, Italy, Poland, and other European
countries sailed to Delaware. They grew
wheat, beans, and corn on the rich, flat
land. They hunted the animals in the
woodlands. Most of the Indians were
pushed off their lands to make room for the settlers. Today,
only a few Nanticoke Indians remain in southern Delaware.

In 1800, a family named du Pont came to Delaware from
France. Eleuthère Irénée du Pont built a gunpowder fac-
tory along Brandywine Creek in 1802. This made him a lot of
money. Soon, the du Pont family branched out into making
cars and chemicals. At one time, half of Delaware's population
worked for a DuPont company. Today, the firm of E. I. du Pont
de Nemours and Company (commonly known as DuPont) is
the largest chemical research facility in the world.

Education helped to improve the lives of many Delawareans. In 1863, Annie Jump Cannon was born in Dover, the
state capital. In her day, most women received no more than
a high school education. But Cannon received undergradu-
ate and graduate degrees from Wellesley College. She then
worked as an astronomer at Harvard University, where
she studied thousands of stars and arranged them into

YEAR

1880   Rehoboth Beach holds what is thought to be the first beauty pageant in the U.S.

EVENT

YEAR

1922   Delaware's first radio station, WDEL, begins broadcasting in Wilmington.

EVENT

categories. Much of what people know about stars today
comes from Cannon's work.

The 1860s were a time of struggle for the U.S. and for
Delaware. One issue that divided many Delawareans was
slavery. Before the Civil War, some people owned black slaves.
In the 1840s, a man named Thomas Garrett risked his life to
provide a safe shelter for slaves escaping from the South. His
home in Wilmington was one of the last stops before slaves
reached freedom in Pennsylvania.

Today, 75 percent of Delaware's population is white.
The next biggest group, at 21 percent, is African American.
Asians and Hispanics come last, but their numbers are
growing. Still, Delaware is near the bottom of all the states
in population size. It is one of the only states to have no city
with a population larger than 100,000. Wilmington is the
largest, with only around 70,000 people.

Although Delaware is America's second-smallest state, it
is diverse. The Chesapeake and Delaware Canal links Chesapeake Bay in Maryland with the Delaware River. The canal is
often thought of as the divider between Delaware's industrial
north and rural south. The northern part is smaller but has
many more people than the south. Most people live in and
around the northern city of Wilmington.

YEAR
1938   The DuPont Company develops nylon, a material used to make parachutes and stockings.
EVENT

Delaware's people are some of the richest in the nation. Its northern cities are home to many of the world's largest corporations. Many people work in banks, chemical companies, or automobile manufacturing. Others work in schools, hospitals, real estate, and stores.

Most of Delaware's farms are located in the central and southern parts of the state. Many farmers grow soybeans and corn, and they raise cattle and broiler chickens. Fishermen catch crabs, clams, and fish. No matter what job they do, Delawareans work hard to make Delaware a great state in which to live.

Those who work in the chemical industry may spend much of their time in laboratories (opposite), while other Delawareans work outside in professions such as fishing for crabs (above).

1951 The Delaware Memorial Bridge opens, spanning the Delaware River and linking Delaware to New Jersey.

Peaches and Pea Patch

DELAWARE'S STATE FLOWER IS THE PEACH BLOSSOM. IN THE 1600S, PEACH TREES GREW ALL OVER THE STATE. PEOPLE DID NOT KNOW WHAT TO DO WITH ALL THE PEACHES. LATER, PEOPLE BEGAN TO SHIP THEM TO OTHER STATES BY STEAMBOATS AND TRAINS. IN 1890, FIVE MILLION PEACH TREES WERE PRODUCING PEACHES IN THE STATE. BUT THEN A DISEASE CAME AND WIPED OUT MANY

of the trees. By 1920, only 500,000 peach trees remained.

Pea Patch Island in the Delaware River is home to Fort Delaware State Park. During the Civil War, the fort served as a prison for captured Confederate soldiers from the South. The prison was damp and cold, and many prisoners died of diseases there. Today, people can ride boats to the park. They walk along the many nature trails on the island. From the top of a tower, people can look out and watch birds nesting.

The du Pont family built many mansions along the Brandywine Creek to show off their wealth. Winterthur and Nemours are two of the big homes. People can tour Winterthur and stroll through its beautiful gardens. Nemours is made of pink stone and looks like a fine European palace.

Peach trees must be pruned yearly (opposite) in order to produce the best fruit (above) and to maintain the health and height of the trees.

YEAR

1971 The state legislature bans the building of industrial plants along the state's coastline.

EVENT

The C-5 Galaxy plane is used by the Air Force to transport troops and supplies in places such as Iraq.

The Hagley Museum sits on the site of the first du Pont gunpowder mill. Many features of the original du Pont mills are preserved there. Visitors can watch an early steam engine and machine shop in action. They can also see how mill workers lived 150 years ago.

The town of New Castle, Delaware's first capital, is the town that time forgot. It looks much as it did more than 300 years ago. Brick buildings line many of the narrow streets. Nearby sits the Dutch House. It was built in the late 1600s and is thought to be the oldest building in the state.

The capital city of Dover houses the largest Air Force base in the eastern U.S. People can look up and see huge C-5 Galaxy airplanes zooming through the skies over Dover. Visitors can tour the base's museum and see aircraft dating back to World War II.

YEAR

1993 Minor league baseball returns to Delaware when the Wilmington Blue Rocks open their season.

EVENT

Historic buildings in cities such as Wilmington (pictured) and New Castle have been carefully restored.

For the first time, U.S. Census data shows that newcomers to Delaware outnumber people born there.

QUICK FACTS

Population: 853,476

Largest city: Wilmington (pop. 72,786)

Capital: Dover

Entered the union: December 7, 1787

Nickname: First State, Blue Hen State

State flower: peach blossom

State bird: blue hen chicken

Size: 2,489 sq mi (6,446 sq km)—2nd-smallest in U.S.

Major industries: manufacturing, farming, banking, fishing, chemicals

People in Delaware like to celebrate the arrival of spring in a unique way. The Great Delaware Kite Festival takes place on the Friday before Easter at Cape Henlopen State Park. People send hundreds of kites soaring into the air.

One of Delaware's biggest festivals is St. Anthony's Festa Italiana. It takes place on the grounds of a Wilmington church in June. Six outdoor cafés are set up. Each café serves a different type of Italian food, such as pizza or cannoli. Each café has a different type of live Italian music, too. Visitors enjoy listening to the music and going on the carnival rides.

The Nanticoke Indians in southern Delaware hold a pow-wow every September. They give demonstrations of their crafts, foods, and customs to all who attend. Visitors also watch ceremonial dancing and listen to storytelling.

People continue to come to Delaware today, to visit or to stay. Its bays and rivers provide great spots for boating, fishing, and swimming. Afterwards, people can eat a delicious seafood dinner fresh from the bay and enjoy a peaceful walk. It is no wonder that so many people never want to leave the welcoming shores of Delaware.

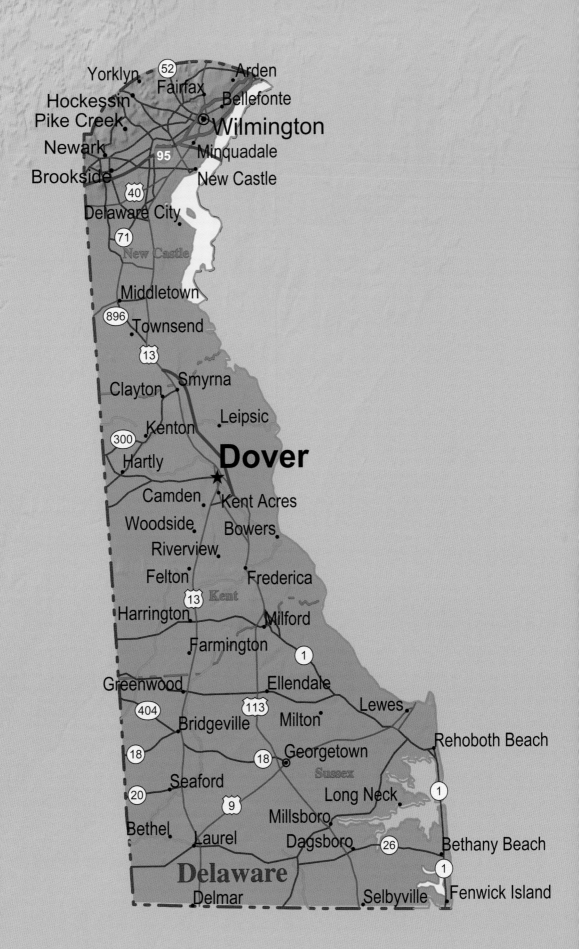

Yorklyn
Fairfax
Arden
Hockessin
Bellefonte
Pike Creek
Wilmington
Newark
Minquadale
Brookside
New Castle
Delaware City
New Castle
Middletown
Townsend
Smyrna
Clayton
Leipsic
Kenton
Dover
Hartly
Camden
Kent Acres
Woodside
Bowers
Riverview
Felton
Frederica
Harrington
Kent
Milford
Farmington
Greenwood
Ellendale
Lewes
Bridgeville
Milton
Rehoboth Beach
Seaford
Georgetown
Sussex
Long Neck
Bethel
Millsboro
Laurel
Dagsboro
Bethany Beach
Delaware
Delmar
Selbyville
Fenwick Island

52
95
40
71
896
13
300
13
1
404
113
18
18
20
9
26
1
1

BIBLIOGRAPHY

Blashfield, Jean F. *Delaware*. New York: Grolier Children's Press, 2000.

Historical Society of Delaware. "Homepage." Delaware History Explorer Online Encyclopedia. http://www.hsd.org/DHE/DHE_welcome.htm.

Miller, Joanne. *Maryland & Delaware*. Emeryville, Calif.: Avalon Travel Publishing, 2001.

San Diego Supercomputer Center. "Annie Jump Cannon." Women in Science. http://www.sdsc.edu/ScienceWomen/cannon.html.

Schuman, Michael. *Delaware*. New York: Benchmark Books, 2000.

State of Delaware. "Homepage." Visit Delaware. http://www.visitdelaware.com/.

INDEX